11/12

# SUPER SKILLS

# ART SKILLS

## STEPHANIE TURNBULL

A⁺
**Smart Apple Media**

Published by Smart Apple Media, an imprint of Black Rabbit Books
P.O. Box 3263, Mankato, Minnesota 56002
www.blackrabbitbooks.com

Printed in the United States of America at Corporate Graphics, North Mankato, Minnesota.

Library of Congress Cataloging-in-Publication Data

Turnbull, Stephanie.
  Art skills / Stephanie Turnbull.
      p. cm. — (Super skills)
  Includes index.
  Summary: "Provides easy-to-follow instructions for many creative art projects including: perspective drawing, photo collage, watercolor painting, and many more. Helps readers develop important artistic skills in a fun and engaging format"—Provided by publisher.
  ISBN 978-1-59920-798-8 (library binding)
  1. Art—Technique—Juvenile literature. I. Title.
  N7440.T87 2013
  702.8—dc23
                            2011040885

Created by Appleseed Editions, Ltd.

Designed and illustrated by Guy Callaby
Edited by Mary-Jane Wilkins
Photo research by Su Alexander

Picture credits
All images are from Shutterstock and Thinkstock apart from the image on page 11 which is from Wikimedia Commons/DIRECTMEDIA/ The Yorck Project.
Cover: Thinkstock

PO1444
2-2012

9 8 7 6 5 4 3 2 1

# CONTENTS

# ARTSY IDEAS

**A**ll you need to create fantastic paintings, drawings, collages, and other artsy projects are a few basic art skills and lots of imagination! This book shows you all kinds of easy techniques and tips to bring out your artistic side.

## What Is Art?

Art is a way of expressing yourself by creating something. It could be a painting, sketch, model, or something completely different—it's up to you!

Some art looks beautiful and some aims to shock or surprise. Images can be amazingly realistic or dramatically distorted. Mastering the skills in this book will help you discover what kind of art you want to make.

# HINTS AND WARNINGS

*In this book, boxes with a lightbulb contain handy hints for making your artwork even better.*

*Boxes with exclamation marks give safety warnings and other important advice.*

◄ ▲ *Two common types of art are portraits of people and **still life** paintings of flowers and other objects. Some artists experiment with shapes and colors to create **abstract** art.*

## Getting Started

Create your own personal space for art projects, whether it's on the kitchen table or in a spare room. Protect surfaces with newspaper or plastic tableclothes, wear an apron or old clothes, and collect all the equipment you need before you begin. Don't rush your work—and remember to clean up afterwards.

▲ *Art supplies may include tubes, bottles, and brushes. Store them somewhere safe.*

◄ *These prehistoric hand paintings were found in Patagonia.*

## SUPER ★ FACTS

★ **The earliest art was prehistoric drawings on cave walls, showing animals and patterns.**

★ **Many modern artists create works called installations that involve viewers by including elements such as sculpture, film, music, and lighting.**

# PAINTING BASICS

**T**here is a huge range of art materials you can buy, but the three easiest paint types to use are watercolors, poster paints, and acrylics. Buy a cheap set of each and see which you prefer.

## What to Use

Watercolors come in tubes or blocks, and are used for landscapes or delicate patterns (see pages 8–9). Poster paints come in squeezy bottles or paintboxes, and can cover big areas with bold colors. Acrylics are fast-drying paints in tubes that are good for painting details or decorating models.

▲ *Watercolors are often sold in boxes that have space for mixing colors.*

◀ *Use acrylic paints straight from the tube, or mix them with water to paint a **wash**.*

## Which Brush?

Buy fat, bristly brushes for poster paint, plus thinner, pointy brushes for watercolor or acrylic details. Clean them with soap and warm water, rinsing until all the paint is gone. Lay them flat to dry.

## Oil Paints

Many artists use oil-based paints because they dry slowly, so there is time to rework sections and blend colors. They're tricky for beginners and also contain solvents that some people are allergic to.

*Acrylic paint is water-resistant when dry, so wash your brushes right away, and try not to get paint on your clothes.*

## Color Choices

Look at a color wheel to help you choose or mix colors for painting. There are three primary colors —red, yellow, and blue. These can be mixed to make other shades, which are called secondary colors. Similar colors are side by side on the wheel. The opposite colors are called complementary colors.

*primary colors*

## Poster Paint Patterns

Here's a great way to experiment with color. Choose similar colors to create subtle shades and shadows, or complementary colors so that each color stands out.

*To darken a color, mix in a little of its complementary color.*

**1.** Stick crisscrossing strips of masking tape on colored card stock.

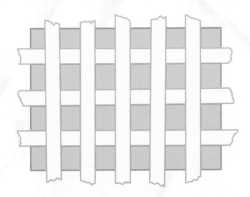

**2.** Cover with poster paint and leave to dry, then carefully peel off the tape.

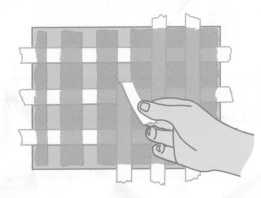

**3.** Stick on new tape strips that overlap the painted squares. Paint with a different color.

**4.** When the paint is dry, peel off the tape. How do your colors look together?

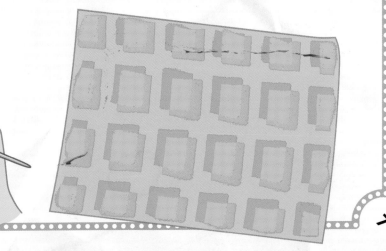

# WATERY EFFECTS

**W**atercolors can be tricky because the paint runs and spreads if it's very watery. You can either paint small sections carefully and let them dry before adding more detail on top, or make everything really wet to create multicolored splotches, swirls, and whirls of blurry color.

## Water Flowers

Painting watercolor patterns on wet paper is an easy way to create beautiful, delicate images. You don't need to worry about getting details just right—the messier the better!

*This watercolor painting has a thin, cloudy background wash under a more detailed image.*

**1.** Wet a thick sheet of paper under the faucet, shake off drips and lay it on newspaper.

**2.** Get lots of paint on a brush and dab it on the paper to make a ring of flower petals. Put blobs of a similar or contrasting color on top, then add other details.

*The colors will spread across the paper.*

**3.** Make more flowers, then leave the paper to dry. Don't move it or the paint will run. Later, cut out your flowers and turn them into gift tags or other decorations.

## Textured Washes

You can use watercolors to make textured patterns. First, paint overlapping strokes of one color across a thick sheet of paper to create a flat wash, or blend several colors for a mix of shades.

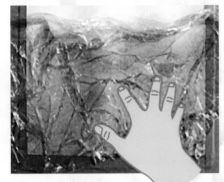

Lay a piece of cling wrap on top of the wet paint. Move it around with your fingertips to mold ridges.

Leave the paint to dry, then peel off the cling wrap. Cut shapes from your textured paper, or use it as the background for a more detailed painting.

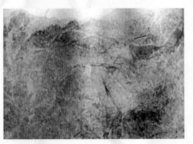

*Blue paint creates the effect of waves or cracked ice, and red can look like rock layers or crumpled parchment.*

Try sprinkling coarse salt on a wet wash. Leave it to dry, then brush off the salt to leave a speckled effect. This happens because salt soaks up the paint around it.

*Salt speckles can create an impression of snow falling or stars in a dark sky.*

# SEEING SPOTS

**W**hen painting with acrylics, try filling in a shape with colored dots. This will help you experiment with colors and think about using lighter and darker shades—which is a great way of making images look real, rather than flat.

## Go Dotty!

To make neat, small paint dots you need a thin brush with a pointed tip. Practice holding the brush steady and making colored dots on paper. Try to make each dot the same size. Another idea is to use a cotton swab dipped in paint, which creates evenly-sized dots.

## Mixing Colors

Dotting colors closely together can create the illusion of blended paint. Make some widely-spaced red dots, let them dry, then add yellow dots in between. From a distance this looks orange. Now try using red and blue to make purple. Experiment with other color combinations.

*Painting with dots takes time! Don't choose big, complicated images, and don't rush, or your dots will get bigger and messier.*

## Dotty Paintings

Choose a photo from a magazine, or study an object. Make sure it's something simple, such as a piece of fruit. Look at the different colors and shades. With a pencil, trace or copy the image on to thick paper and lightly map out areas of different shades.

brown

light area

dark area

green

*Erase the pencil lines when the paint is dry.*

Choose a few colors and start filling the shape with tiny dots. In lighter areas, place the dots far apart. To show darker areas, put the dots closer together or add other colors in between to make interesting shades.

## More Ideas

Dots make great patterns. Sketch a design first, then go over it with dots. Start at the far side of the paper and work towards yourself, so you don't smudge the paint as you work. You could also try using small dashes instead of dots.

## SUPER ★ FACTS

★ The technique of painting using dots is called pointillism.

★ Pointillism was developed by the French artist Georges Seurat (1859–91). He wanted to make colors stand out vividly.

▶ *A pointillist painting by Georges Seurat called* The Circus.

*Le Cirque by Georges Seurat in Musée d'Orsay*

# SPLAT!

**W**ho says you need to paint with a brush? Some artists create paintings by pouring or dripping paint, or even flinging it from a distance then rolling around on the **canvas**! If you don't want to get quite that messy, try these great methods of applying paint.

## Paint Flicking Fun

Splattering paint on colored paper with a toothbrush is fun and very effective. Make sure you have lots of space so you don't spray the furniture!

**1.** Squeeze some poster paint into a bowl and add a little water so it's runny. Find an old toothbrush, a small square of thick cardboard, and some colored paper.

*Always scrape towards yourself, or you'll flick paint on your clothes.*

**2.** Dip the toothbrush in paint and scrape the cardboard across it, so the paint sprays over the paper. Experiment with different colored paints and paper to see what looks good.

**3.** When it's dry, cut out shapes to make pictures. Try a bright seaside scene with speckled sandcastles and a sparkling sea.

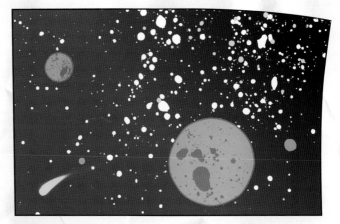

Or try a starry night sky with fantastic planets.

*Smudge a blob of paint with your finger to add a shooting star!*

## Splotch Monsters

You can use runny poster paint to make brilliant blobby aliens, with the help of a drinking straw.

**1.** Drop a little paint onto a sheet of paper. Carefully blow the paint outwards with a straw to make strange shapes.

*Mix cornstarch into paint to thicken it, then drag cardboard shapes or sticks through it to make textured patterns.*

**2.** When the paint is dry, add small details with a marker or acrylic paint.

# PERFECT PRINTS

**M**aking prints with cutout shapes is another way to apply paint without a brush. You could frame your prints, create sheets of customized wrapping paper, or even put your design on a t-shirt using fabric paints.

## Printing Materials

Artists make prints with materials such as wood, **linoleum**, rubber, or metal. They cut or carve around a design, cover the raised image with ink, and press it down onto paper or cloth.

Try this with a potato. Cut it in half, draw a simple shape, then carefully cut away the potato around the shape. This works with sponges, too.

▲ *Use big, bold designs and bright colors to create stylish prints, like this woodcut of a tree.*

Another method is to use materials with interesting textures, like bubble wrap. Cut out shapes, cover them in thick paint, then press them onto paper.

▲ *Potato prints are ideal for decorating your own Christmas cards and gift tags.*

## Food Prints

A Japanese printing technique called gyotaku involves painting fish with ink, then pressing paper on top to create prints. Try using apple, orange, or lemon halves instead of a fish to create rows of brightly colored shapes.

*Practice on scrap paper to figure out how much paint to use. If there is too much, you won't see delicate patterns.*

*Be extremely careful when using a knife. Always cut away from yourself, and ask for help if you need it.*

## Fingerprint Animals

Hand, foot, and fingerprints make great textured images. Try creating funny fingerprint animals. Let your prints dry before drawing in extra details.

Try some ants…          …a robin…          …or a long caterpillar.

# CREATIVE COLLAGE

**A** collage is a collection of materials glued on the page to create a piece of art. Collages can be made of paper, fabric, buttons, string, bark, pasta, or candy. It's entirely up to you! See what you can find to recycle into a collage.

## Collage Effects

The great thing about collage is that you can do what you like with your materials —cut them, tear them, scrunch, or twist them! Space things out across the page or layer them thickly. Mix materials or add a collage to a painting to give it an interesting texture.

*Don't be impatient to start gluing! Try arranging things in different positions on the page before you stick them down.*

## SUPER ★ FACTS

★ The term "collage" comes from the French word coller, which means "to glue."

★ Famous artists who experimented with collage include Georges Braque (1882–1963) and Pablo Picasso (1881–1973).

## Focus the Eye

Don't make your collage too busy or too bland. Large scenes look better if there is something striking to focus on.

For example, use overlapping strips of tissue paper to create a tranquil beach scene.

Then add a few carefully-placed details as a focus to hold the scene together.

## Striking Silhouettes

Another way to create an eye-catching collage is to use silhouettes.

**1.** Cut building shapes from black paper. Make holes for windows.

**2.** Arrange the buildings on tracing paper and glue them down. Hang the picture in front of a lamp to illuminate your city scene.

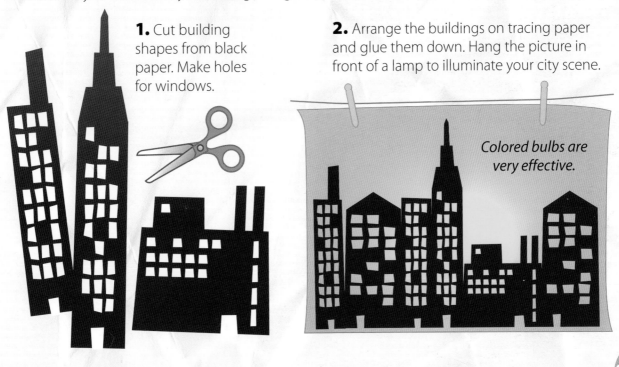

*Colored bulbs are very effective.*

# FUN WITH PHOTOS

**C**reate striking effects with photographs. Use prints of images you've taken yourself, or pictures cut from magazines. Mix and match parts of photos to create collages that are **surreal**, surprising, or downright silly!

## Crazy Cutting

Collect a pile of large, interesting photos, cut them up, and experiment with reassembling the pieces in a different order. This technique is called cubomania.

You could also cut a photo into strips, then stick the strips on paper with a gap between each.

*This emphasizes the giraffe's long neck.*

Why not combine two photos? Choose two similar shapes for a funny effect.

## Ugly Mugs

The technique of making collages from photos is called photomontage. This works well with faces cut from magazines. Draw a head shape, then choose eyes, eyebrows, a nose, mouth, and so on. Pick a variety of sizes and shapes. Cut or tear squares of skin and hair to complete the face.

## Dreamscapes

Another great photomontage idea is to combine images to form a dreamlike picture. Find a large photo of a landscape—like mountains or a desert —then add objects and people. Vary sizes and put unusual things together. The more surreal, the better!

*The eyes should be about halfway down a realistic head, but you can distort proportions to make really odd faces.*

Make a dream landscape look even more bizarre by turning over an image, so the writing or images on the back are showing.

# DRAWING BASICS

**W**hen you're feeling creative, you should never be without a pencil for doodling, sketching, or creating complete drawings. Most drawings are done on paper, using **graphite** pencils, ink, crayons, charcoal, chalk, or pastels.

## Pencil Types

Pencils are graded according to how hard (H) or soft (B for black) the graphite is—9H is very hard, 9B very soft, and HB somewhere in the middle. Use hard pencils for sharp, grey lines in detailed, precise drawings. Choose softer pencils for sketching, when you want to blur lines, or make shadows.

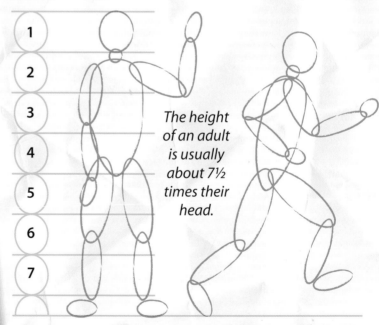

## Size and Shade

Drawings look more realistic if everything is in proportion. This means making objects the right size and shape in relation to each other. Another useful technique is shading—filling in darker areas to create shadows and make objects look three-dimensional.

*Find a good eraser that doesn't smudge. Artists buy squishy, washable erasers that don't leave pieces behind.*

1
2
3
4
5
6
7

*The height of an adult is usually about 7½ times their head.*

*Use this guide for drawing people. Sketch simple shapes first to get the proportions right.*

## Perspective

Another way of making drawings look realistic is to use perspective. This means creating a sense of depth and distance, for example by making objects smaller if they are far away. Here's how to draw a simple scene in **one-point perspective**. You'll need a ruler.

**1.** Draw a line across a piece of paper for the horizon. Mark a point in the middle. This is called the vanishing point.

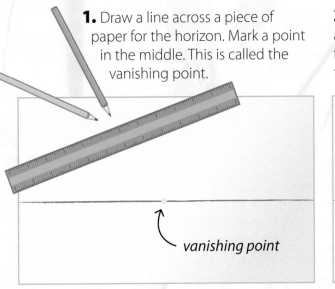

*vanishing point*

**2.** Draw an object, such as a tree, to the left of the picture. Now draw faint lines from the top and bottom of the tree, leading to the vanishing point.

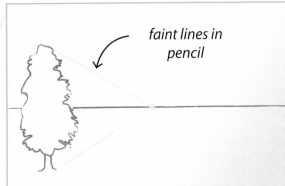

*faint lines in pencil*

**3.** Use these guidelines to draw more trees in a line. They get smaller towards the vanishing point, although in real life they would be the same size.

**4.** Try adding a wall or train track using similar guidelines. Experiment with other scenes, like a street with houses on each side, or a hallway with pictures on the walls.

*Erase the guidelines when you're finished.*

## Breaking the Rules

Although these drawing techniques are useful, don't despair if you find them tricky. Remember, many artists create fantastic works by drawing deliberately nonproportional people and impossible perspectives!

# CARTOONS

Cartoon characters are fun to look at and even more fun to draw. Use a soft pencil and sketch shapes faintly, then press harder when you've found the line you want. You can erase the lines you don't need, or trace over your finished character for a clean copy.

## Cheeky Faces

There are many ways to draw cartoon faces, but here's one method to get you started.

**1.** First, sketch two ovals.

**2.** Add the eyes, nose, mouth, ear, hairline, and neck.

**3.** Use these guidelines to go over the final face.

Try using this basic face shape to experiment with different expressions. The position of the mouth and eyebrows make all the difference—try it and see! Next, add speech bubbles and make a comic strip with your invented characters.

WHICH SIDE OF A LEOPARD HAS THE MOST SPOTS?

I DON'T KNOW

THE OUTSIDE!!

G R O A N

# Crazy Creatures

Animals make great cartoons. Play around with different features and expressions to make them cute, angry, tired, or dopey. Here's a greedy dog to try.

**1.** Sketch two ovals for the head and body, and add a nose and ears.

**2.** Add the eyes, mouth, legs, feet, tail, and the bone the dog is chasing. Keep all the shapes very simple.

**3.** Add other details and go over the lines to make your final dog.

*Soft pencils smudge easily, so don't rest your hand on your work as you draw!*

# Dino Designs

Dinosaurs are easy to draw. Roughly sketch one of these simple designs as the basic body shape. Now invent extra features, like spikes or horns. Make the shapes fatter, thinner, or longer and create facial expressions.

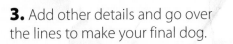

# COMPUTER ART

**C**omputers can help you create all kinds of artsy effects. Some artists scan their work and alter or add to it on screen, while others use computer programs to create intricate designs and patterns.

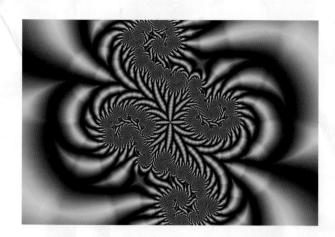

## Digital Portraits

One effective way of creating computer art is to manipulate photographs.

▲ *This complicated pattern of swirls and curves is called a fractal and was created on a computer.*

**1.** First, find a digital photo of a person, for example, a friend, a movie star, or yourself. Copy and paste it into a blank document.

**2.** Use the picture toolbar to make the image black and white and increase the contrast so the dark areas stand out.

**3.** Copy the photo and paste it into a program like Microsoft Paint, with a colored background. Paste lots of copies to build up a page of tessellating tiles —shapes that fit together with no gaps or overlap.

**4.** Experiment by changing the photo colors.

## Tessellations

Computers are ideal for creating all kinds of complicated tessellations. To try this, open a program like Microsoft Paint.

Get inspiration from the work of the Dutch artist M. C. Escher (1898–1972), who created amazing animal and bird tessellations.

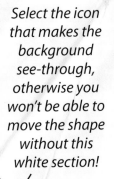

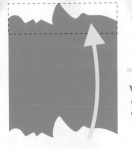

Select the icon that makes the background see-through, otherwise you won't be able to move the shape without this white section!

**1.** Select the solid rectangle tool and draw a rectangle or square, then fill it with color.

**2.** Cut a wiggly section from the bottom of the shape using the free-form select tool.

**3.** Move the cutout section to the top of the shape. Don't leave a gap.

**4.** Now cut out a section from the left and move it to the right of the shape.

**5.** Go to the select tool (a box of dotted lines) and draw a box around the new shape. Copy and paste it, then change the color. Move it to line up with the first shape.

**6.** Add more shapes in the same way to fill the page!

Andy Warhol
2002          USA **37**

★ The American artist Andy Warhol (1928–87) was famous for using painting, printing, and computer manipulation to color black and white portraits.

**SUPER ★ FACTS**

★ Some computer artists make pictures using lines of type, altering the color and shade of letters to make patterns down the page. Try it yourself!

25

# BODY ART

**H**ow about creating artistic images on yourself or a friend? Some artists paint faces, hands, nails, or even whole bodies! If you want to try body art, buy special face or body paints. Never use ordinary paint as this will damage your skin.

▲ *Face and body paints are water-based, so they wash off easily with soap and water.*

*Some people are allergic to face and body paint. Try a small amount first to make sure it doesn't irritate the skin, and never paint on sore or broken skin.*

## Get Cheeky!

Cheek designs are a good way to get started with body art. Simple images work well, like butterflies, stars, balloons, or flowers. Draw just on the cheek or curve your design around the eye and down the side of the face.

**1.** A spider's web is great for a Halloween party. Use a thin, pointed brush and start by drawing a curved white diamond.

**2.** Add lines from each point of the diamond, and from the middle of each line.

**3.** Join the lines with curved webbing.

*Sprinkle on body glitter (NOT ordinary glitter) to make your web shimmer.*

**4.** Paint black ovals for the spider's head and body and make eight bold brush strokes for legs. Add red eyes.

## Full Faces

To paint a whole face, you need sponges for covering large areas. They often come with face painting kits, or you can buy them separately. Try this tiger face.

**1.** Put yellow paint on a damp sponge and dab a thin wash over the center of the face.

**2.** Sponge around the outside of the face with orange. Blend the colors where they join.

*Be careful not to get paint in the eyes.*

**3.** Use a brush to paint white spiky eyebrows and cheek stripes. Paint a white patch of pointy whiskers around the mouth area.

★ An Italian artist, Guido Daniele, paints hands to look like amazingly realistic bird and animal heads.

★ There is a long South Asian tradition of painting intricate patterns on hands and feet using a reddish-brown dye called henna (below). People often wear henna for weddings.

**4.** Paint the tip of the nose black and draw a line down to the top lip. Add black dots and whiskers above the mouth and outline the patch under the bottom lip. Paint black cheek stripes between the white ones.

# WHAT NEXT?

**O**nce you've tried the techniques in this book, keep working on those you like best. Are you happiest working with paints, pencils, collage, or computers? The more you practice, the better you'll become, and you'll begin to develop a personal style too.

## Explore Art

Visit art galleries and exhibitions and keep an open mind about what you like —you may be surprised. Take a notebook and jot down ideas. Experiment with techniques and materials, and don't be disappointed if something doesn't turn out right—it may lead to a better idea.

► *Some art is designed to be studied. Look at how artists use colors and textures.*

▼ *Some skills need special supplies like cameras, pens, ceramic tiles, or clay sculpting tools.*

## Try New Things

There are many art skills to try. Why not look for local classes teaching photography, **calligraphy,** or sculpture? If you're serious about studying art, read up on college and university art and design courses. Enter competitions and find out whether you can exhibit your work at local galleries, libraries, or coffee shops.

Extend your creative skills by trying craft techniques like weaving, modeling, **origami**, and mask-making. Another book in this series, Craft Skills, will give you great ideas!

## Artistic Careers

A passion for art can lead to all kinds of careers. How about being an architect, florist, **stonemason,** or furniture maker? You could bring drawings to life as an animator, create special effects for films or plays, design complicated websites, or even teach art to others.

◀ ▲ *Maybe you see yourself working as a book illustrator in your own studio (above), or perhaps applying dramatic makeup to film stars, theater actors, or fashion models (left).*

# GLOSSARY

**abstract**
A piece of art that doesn't show people, places, or ordinary objects, but instead uses colors and shapes to suggest ideas or emotions.

**calligraphy**
Beautiful, decorative handwriting or lettering.

**canvas**
A thick, woven fabric on which many artists paint.

**fabric paints**
Paints that are designed to be used on textiles; they print best on natural fibers like cotton and linen.

**graphite**
A soft, dark type of carbon that is mixed with clay to make lead for pencils.

**linoleum**
A thick, long-lasting material made by coating a sheet of canvas with a mixture that includes oil and powdered cork.

**one-point perspective**
A type of drawing in which all diagonal lines meet at a single "vanishing point" on the horizon; more complicated perspective drawings can have many vanishing points.

**origami**
A Japanese art of folding paper to create beautiful models.

**still life**
A piece of art showing an arrangement of non-moving objects, for example a vase of flowers or a bowl of fruit.

**stonemason**
A person skilled in carving blocks of stone (to make statues or monuments), or laying and fitting stone into place as part of building projects.

**surreal**
Putting unusual or surprising images together in a bizarre, dreamlike way.; surrealism is an imaginative style of art and writing that began in the early 1920s.

**wash**
A smooth, thin layer of watery paint.

# USEFUL WEBSITES

**www.watercolorpainting.com/watercolor-tutorials.htm**
Find tutorials for creating many kinds of washes and effects with watercolors at this site.

**www.dianewrightfineart.com/tutorials.htm**
Let renowned pencil artist Diane Wright teach you pencil techniques with her online tutorials.

**www.activitytv.com/cartooning-for-kids**
Watch short, easy-to-follow videos that show you how to draw wacky cartoons.

**www.tessellations.org**
Browse a whole site dedicated to tessellations. Look at great examples of tessellating pictures, learn more about M. C. Escher, and find out how to make your own brilliant tessellations.

**www.artschools.com/careers-jobs**
Find out more about careers in art, including exciting job profiles of graphic designers, photographers, fashion designers, and many other artistic jobs.